INTRODUCTION
TO
THUMB POSITION

(Cello)

A. W. BENOY
and
L. SUTTON

MUSIC DEPARTMENT

OXFORD
UNIVERSITY PRESS

INTRODUCTION TO THUMB POSITION
(Cello)

by A. W. Benoy and L. Sutton

PART I

(No extensions or changes in the position of the thumb required)

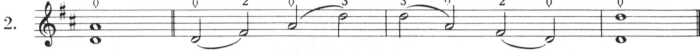

Franconia

Czech Folk Song

Scottish Dance
(There's nae luck)

Part II (for which extensions and changes in the position of the thumb are required) is on page 11

Irish Love Song

(Believe me, if all those endearing young charms)

Exercise

Gaelic Lullaby

Scandinavian Dance

(Cochin China)

To Wander

10. Allegro — Schubert

11.

12.

Old French Carol
(La Ballade de Jésus Christ)

13. Andante

Old French Carol
(Noël Nouvelet)

14. Andante

Shepherds' Song
(from Quintet, L' Uccelliera)

15. Andante Pastorale — Boccherini

English Folk Song
(The Tailor and the Mouse)

Pavane

Arbeau

6

Peaceful Slumbering Ocean

Storace

Hornpipe

The Dashing White Sergeant

How blest are shepherds
(King Arthur)

Purcell

25.

Staines Morris

26.

Country Dance

27.

Gavotte

Mozart

28.

Polka

London New

Ecossaise

Beethoven

May Song

Trumpet Tune
(King Arthur)

Purcell

Savez-vous planter les choux

Duke Street

Bohemian Waltz
(Der Freischütz)

Weber

PART II

(Extensions and changes in the position of the thumb required)

Country Dance
(The Pirates' Waltz)

German Folk Song
(Be kind, gentle Shepherdess)

Contentment

Mozart

German Folk Song

(Awake, my heart's desire)

Scottish Traditional Song

(A Rosebud by my early walk)

Country Dance

(The Phoenix)

14

Minuet

Handel

Country Dance
(The Devil among the Tailors)

Country Dance
(The Marquis of Lorne)

Cradle Song

Andante tranquillo

Schubert

57.

He shall feed his flock

(Messiah)

Larghetto

Handel

58.

Allegretto

(Octet in E)

Allegretto

Spohr

59.

La Pastourelle

Couperin

The Little Spinner

Mozart

Andante

(Symphony No. 2)

Schubert

Reproduced and printed by
Halstan & Co. Ltd., Amersham, Bucks., England